Chocoholic Reasonettes

Little Excuses to Eat Chocolate!

by Sherrie Weaver

Introduction

In reality, it is much more difficult to come up with reasons NOT to eat chocolate than it is to think of reasons to indulge. This book is the result of grueling preparation and intense research, which I enjoyed immensely. I visited candy shops, grocery stores and specialty shops, justifying it all by telling people I was doing research for a book. No one believed me, of course, but I had a great time anyway. My complexion is shot, my jeans won't button and I owe money to every candy store in town. Which leads me to my next book…365 Diet Tips for Chocoholics.

This book is dedicated to Jessica and Seth, who have both given me really good reasons to eat chocolate. To Mom and Lynn, who always have chocolate available and to Shadow, Bluebelly, and Spud, who have tried since they were puppies to get me to share my chocolate.

Cover Illustration by Design Dynamics
Typography by MarketForce

Published by Great Quotations Publishing Co,
8102 Lemont Road, #300
Woodridge, IL 60517

Library of Congress Catalog Card Number: 97-77639

ISBN 1-56245-334-3

Printed in Hong Kong 2005

The most popular flavor
for those diet shake drinks
is chocolate.
That ought to tell
us something.

4

Chocoholic Reasonettes

**Chocolate will get you
through times of no money,
but money will not get you
through times of no chocolate.**

5

5% of women crave chocolate after sex.
The other 95% crave chocolate
instead of sex.

If someone would
invent chocolate toothpaste,
this whole dental hygiene
thing would be a lot
easier to swallow.

7

Chocoholic Reasonettes

**An oxymoron:
Leftover chocolate.**

Chocoholic Reasonettes

**Woman does not live
by chocolate alone.
She needs ice cream, too.**

Chocoholic Reasonettes

**If you have dogs in the house,
it is your duty to eat all the chocolate,
since it is toxic to dogs.**

Chocoholic Reasonettes

The way to a man's heart
is through his stomach.
The way to a woman's heart
is through her sweet tooth.

Chocoholic Reasonettes

Dip teaspoons in melted
chocolate and chill.
Then use them
for stirring coffee.

12

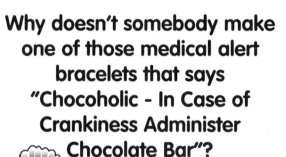

Why doesn't somebody make one of those medical alert bracelets that says "Chocoholic - In Case of Crankiness Administer Chocolate Bar"?

When they say vitamin C,
do they mean chocolate?

Chocoholic Reasonettes

I'd sing the praises of chocolate...
except my mouth's full.

15

**Chocolate -
The world's best
over-the-counter
anti-depressant.**

16

If chocolate is a problem for you,
try aversion therapy.
Eat nothing but chocolate.
After 6 or 7 years,
you'll get tired of it.

If you've got melted
chocolate all over your hands,
you're eating it
too slowly.

If you drink too much beer,
you get a hangover.
If you eat too much chocolate,
you just hang
over your belt.

**You might be
a chocoholic if:
You've ever had
a 'shooter' of
chocolate syrup.**

20

Chocoholic Reasonettes

"Death by chocolate..."
Now that's capital
punishment
I can live with.

21

Chocoholic Reasonettes

Pour melted chocolate into
an ice cream cone before filling.
While it's still soft, add some peanuts.

22

**Flowers and candy?
Just forget the flowers and spend
twice as much on candy.**

Chocoholic Reasonettes

Guys, bring the candy before
you do something wrong.
Afterwards, it's too late.

Chocoholic Reasonettes

A hollow chocolate Easter bunny
is like a plain cake donut.
It'll do in a pinch,
but it would be much better
with something in the middle.

**"The road to hell is
paved with good intentions."**
The road to heaven is paved with chocolate.

Chocoholic Reasonettes

**A good chocolate bar is like a symphony —
meant to be savored slowly
and with great gusto.**

27

The phrase 'good chocolate' is a redundancy.

28

**The best cure for PMS
is a load of chocolate in the
hands of a contrite male.**

29

Even the worst chocolate bar
is 100 times better than
the best gumdrop.

**Wouldn't it be great if
'chocolate bar' was a place,
like a sports bar or
a cowboy bar?**

31

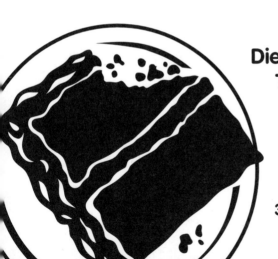

**Diet chocolate is here —
The Weight is over!**

32

Carob is chocolate's evil twin.

Sugar free chocolate
is the non-alcoholic beer
of the candy world.

Chocoholic Reasonettes

**Try adding chopped up
peanut butter cups to peanut
butter cookie dough before baking.**

Who says chocolate
isn't good for you?
It sure makes me feel better.

Chocoholic Reasonettes

Chocolate covered raisins,
cherries, orange slices &
strawberries all count as fruit,
so eat as many
as you want.

Chocoholic Reasonettes

Nuts have protein,
and protein is necessary for life.
So eat some chocolate covered
peanuts before it's too late.

**The problem:
how to get 2 pounds of chocolate
home from the store in a hot car.
The solution:
eat it in the parking lot.**

For a beautiful, edible garnish,
use a paintbrush to paint
melted chocolate
onto mint leaves.

40

You might be a chocoholic if:
you've ever fantasized
about being encased in
a block of chocolate
and eating
your way free.

41

**Diet tip:
eat a chocolate bar
before each meal.
It'll take the edge off
your appetite and
you'll eat less.**

42

I would enjoy football much more
if instead of the 'beer man',
they had a 'chocolate man'
at the stadium.

43

Chocoholic Reasonettes

**If it's really hot outside,
you can drink
your chocolate bar
and save time.**

44

Chocoholic Reasonettes

**Chocolate stores best
at about 60 degrees.
Problem is,
why would you
want to store it?**

A nice box of chocolates
can provide your total daily
intake of calories,
all in one place.
Isn't that handy?

**Burn some calories
without giving up chocolate.
Keep your supply in the attic,
so that you have to climb
stairs to get some.**

Chocoholic Reasonettes

**You might be a chocoholic if:
You've ever had to give out little
baggies of chow mein noodles
for Halloween because you've
eaten all the 'Fun Size'
candy bars.**

48

Personally, I believe chocolate is God's way of making up for okra.

If you can't eat all your chocolate
it will keep in the freezer.
But if you can't eat all your chocolate,
what is wrong with you?

Chocoholic Reasonettes

That chocolate bar took thousands of
dollars in labor and effort to produce,
and yet the store only wants
95 cents for it.
How can you pass up
a bargain like that?

51

Chocoholic Reasonettes

If calories are an issue,
store your chocolate
on top of the fridge.
Calories are afraid of heights,
and they will jump out
of the chocolate to
protect themselves.

52

Once you've eaten chocolate
it's all 'behind' you.

53

You might be a chocoholic if:
You walk into a candy store
and order 'the usual'.

Never give medicine to a child by
camouflaging it in chocolate.
They'll want to be
sick all the time.

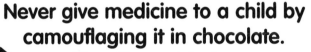

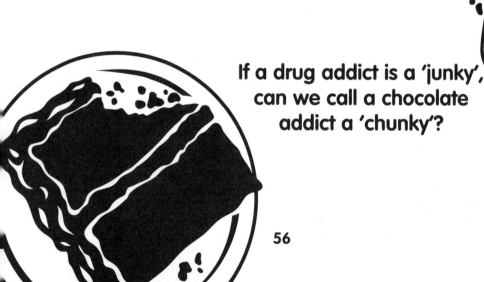

Chocoholic Reasonettes

If a drug addict is a 'junky',
can we call a chocolate
addict a 'chunky'?

Chocoholic Reasonettes

The average woman eats 4 lbs of chocolate a year. You can do better, girl.

Chocoholic Reasonettes

**Spoiled fruit draws flies.
Chocolate never hangs around
long enough to spoil.**

**I don't drink coffee.
Can I have a chocolate
break instead?**

Chocoholic Reasonettes

Never trust anyone who can eat only half a candy bar.

Chocoholic Reasonettes

**What is the big deal
about chocolate?
If I have to explain it,
you wouldn't understand it.**

Chocoholic Reasonettes

**Chocolate will help make
Mondays bearable.
(If you eat enough of it!)**

Chocoholic Reasonettes

You may be a chocoholic if:
you've ever licked all the
chocolate frosting off of a donut
and then put it back on the tray
trying to pass it off as 'glazed'.

Chocoholic Reasonettes

**Small children do not
generally appreciate the
true worth of chocolate.
You should eat their
Halloween candy.**

64

My chocolate or my money.....
well, I can always earn
more money.

65

Why can't the people
who manufacture chocolate
take over the government?
Then everything would
be smooth and sweet.

Chocoholic Reasonettes

**If a candy bar is broken,
all the calories leak out.**

When all else fails, chocolate won't.

Chocoholic Reasonettes

Chocolate cannot save
a troubled relationship,
but it can certainly
take your mind off
it for awhile.

Chocoholic Reasonettes

You might be a chocoholic if:
during word association,
someone says 'dark',
and you respond with 'milk'.

Chocoholic Reasonettes

Chocolate contains sugar,
which is made from vegetables.
It has milk, which comes from cows.
Where else can you find
so much healthy stuff
packed into one treat?

Why isn't there a statue dedicated to the guy who invented chocolate?

Chocoholic Reasonettes

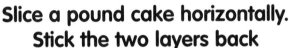

Slice a pound cake horizontally.
Stick the two layers back
together with chocolate
frosting and drizzle
with chocolate syrup.

If Marie Antoinette had said,
"Let them eat <u>chocolate</u> cake",
she'd have been fine.

Chocoholic Reasonettes

Always keep an extra
chocolate bar in the first aid kit,
in case of emergencies.

**If I eat equal amounts of
dark chocolate and white chocolate,
is that a balanced diet?**

76

**Employee Relations:
If I don't get my chocolate,
you don't get
your work done.**

77

Chocolate coated coffee beans
are as close to a perfect
food as we can get.

**Keep some variety in your life.
Buy assorted chocolates.**

Chocoholic Reasonettes

**Give chocolate
to your friends.
Then they'll gain weight
and make you
look wonderful.**

Chocoholic Reasonettes

**Chocolate is
worth weighting for.**

A 5 pound box of chocolates - weight lifting.

Chocoholic Reasonettes

You might be a chocoholic if:
you think there should be
a transferral patch for
chocolate cravings.

83

Chocoholic Reasonettes

You really want to attract a woman? Try chocolate aftershave.

Chocoholic Reasonettes

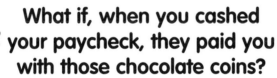

What if, when you cashed
your paycheck, they paid you
with those chocolate coins?

Chocoholic Reasonettes

**Ever get tired of chocolate?
Do you ever get tired of breathing?**

My chocolate has gone to waist.

Chocoholic Reasonettes

It's cheaper to celebrate
a special occasion with chocolate
than with champagne.

88

Chocoholic Reasonettes

If you're too sick to eat chocolate, you should be in the hospital.

Make a chocolate taco with waffles,
chocolate pudding
and whipped cream.

Chocoholic Reasonettes

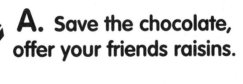

Q. Three friends, two chocolate bars, what do you do?

A. Save the chocolate, offer your friends raisins.

Chocoholic Reasonettes

If the wedding cake were chocolate, the bride would shove it into her own mouth.

Chocoholic Reasonettes

You're not pigging out, you're in training for a chocolate consumption test.

93

**If the dark clouds were chocolate,
we'd all be hoping for rain.**

**Teach your kids not to eat chocolate.
You don't need the competition.**

Chocoholic Reasonettes

Ever stayed in a fancy hotel just for the little chocolates they put on your pillow?

96

Money talks. Chocolate sings.

Life is bowl of chocolate-covered cherries.

**Eating chocolate is the one thing
you will never forget to do.**

It could be worse.
You could be out of chocolate.
If you are out of chocolate,
just give up.

**Quick, fax me
some chocolate.**

101

Chocoholic Reasonettes

You may be a chocoholic if:
there is an entry in your household
budget for chocolate,
and it's 3 figures.

Chocoholic Reasonettes

I've got to cut back on
my chocolate consumption.
Eventually.

103

Chocoholic Reasonettes

A day without chocolate is pointless.

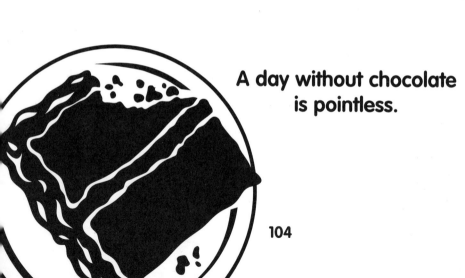

104

Chocoholic Reasonettes

I never met a piece
of fudge I didn't like.

Chocoholic Reasonettes

Fat-free chocolate is for wimps.

Chocoholic Reasonettes

A cup of chocolate has just as
much caffeine as a cup of coffee,
and it is more fun to consume.
Coffee gets cold.
Chocolate is meant to be
served at room temperature.

Chocoholic Reasonettes

**Avoid clutter.
Don't leave chocolate
lying around.**

Chocolate was once
considered an aphrodisiac.
Hey, it couldn't hurt.

109

Chocoholic Reasonettes

**Years ago, only the very wealthy
could afford chocolate.
Live well, eat lots.**

Chocoholic Reasonettes

You don't have to ask
permission from anybody.
You can have as much
chocolate as you want.
Go for it.

Chocoholic Reasonettes

You're going to
have a busy day,
so you're going to
need the extra energy
that chocolate gives.

**Chocolate is the only
anti-depressant that is
not regulated by
the federal government.**

113

If you gain enough weight,
you will need a
whole new wardrobe.

Chocoholic Reasonettes

Chocolate has many preservatives.
Preservatives make
you look younger.

115

You get to practice your Will Power everyday. Let your Won't Power have a turn.

Chocoholic Reasonettes

**Celebrate diversity!
Eat white chocolate,
dark chocolate
and milk chocolate.**

117

Chocoholic Reasonettes

If John Belushi, Elvis and Jimi Hendrix had made chocolate their drug of choice, they might still be with us.

All men are created equal.
But some of them know
how to make brownies.

Chocoholic Reasonettes

Keep a chocolate dish on your desk, and you will be the center of office communications.

120

Chocoholic Reasonettes

If you deny yourself chocolate,
you will damage your own
self-esteem and probably
commit some kind of
gruesome crime.

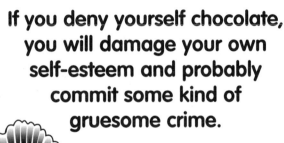

Chocoholic Reasonettes

With a belly full of chocolate,
you will have no room for
high fat, high sodium cheeseburgers.

Chocoholic Reasonettes

**If you don't gain weight in the winter time,
you won't be able to take part
in that Spring-time diet frenzy.**

Chocoholic Reasonettes

If we don't eat chocolate,
the folks who produce it
will lose their jobs.
Do you want the downfall of
our nation's economy
on your shoulders?

124

Chocoholic Reasonettes

Chocolate never puts you on hold.

125

Chocoholic Reasonettes

Wouldn't you just love to throttle whoever thought of putting the calorie content on chocolate bar wrappers?

126

Chocoholic Reasonettes

Eat your chocolate now,
before you lose all your teeth
and have to substitute
chocolate syrup.

127

Chocoholic Reasonettes

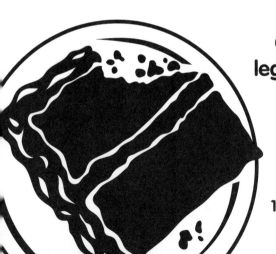

**Chocolate is cheap,
legal and non-alcoholic.**

128

Chocoholic Reasonettes

**Gain weight
from chocolate?
Fat chance.**

129

We can't smoke or drink at work,
but there is always the candy machine.

No animals were killed to make chocolate.

**Chocolate is the
sweet spot in my day.**

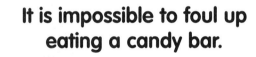

It is impossible to foul up eating a candy bar.

Chocoholic Reasonettes

If chocolate reaches
it's expiration date,
it will get thrown away.
It's bad to waste food.

Chocoholic Reasonettes

You may be a chocoholic if:
you can eat the chocolate
from around the peanut butter
part of the peanut butter cup.

Chocoholic Reasonettes

**Fruit generally has either a
peel or a core to dispose of.
Chocolate doesn't.
So if you eat chocolate,
you won't be adding
to our landfill
problems.**

Chocoholic Reasonettes

**Would you rather have
your teenage daughter
make fudge or kiss a boy?**

137

Nicotine can kill.
Sex can kill. Liquor can kill.
At least chocolate is safe.

Chocoholic Reasonettes

**Everybody is losing weight.
Be a rebel; gain some.**

Chocoholic Reasonettes

Eat it now, before global warming melts it all.

140

No such thing as 'second hand' chocolate fumes.

You have to indulge yourself.
Odds are good that you're
the only one who will.

Eating chocolate doesn't make you a pig.
Four legs and a curly tail,
now that makes you a pig.

Chocoholic Reasonettes

Chocolate is not a substitute for friendship. But it will also never borrow $20 from you.

144

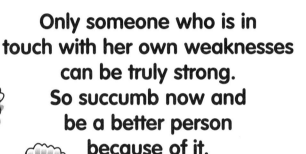

Chocoholic Reasonettes

Only someone who is in touch with her own weaknesses can be truly strong. So succumb now and be a better person because of it.

145

Chocoholic Reasonettes

**Why not eat chocolate?
It's more fun than your job.**

**There are other things
in life besides chocolate.
But none of them really matter.**

Chocoholic Reasonettes

As much time as you spend at work,
you'll never have to worry
about what you look like
in a bikini, anyway.

148

**Chocolate will never
keep you waiting in traffic.**

Chocoholic Reasonettes

Q. Why is there no such organization as Chocoholics Anonymous?

A. Because no one wants to quit.

**If you have chocolate
in your hand,
you will be unable
to do your job.
So eat it and
get to work.**

151

Chocoholic Reasonettes

You can buy chocolate
without showing your ID.

152

Chocoholic Reasonettes

**Eat healthy.
Die anyway.**

153

Winter is coming.
You'll need the extra insulation
that fat gives.

Chocoholic Reasonettes

If you leave that chocolate around,
your kids could eat it and
develop a weight problem.
You don't want that on
your conscience, do you?

A spoonful of sugar makes
the medicine go down.
A spoonful of chocolate
keeps it there.

Chocoholic Reasonettes

Chocolate has no moving parts or sharp edges.

Chocolate is a serious snack.
So quit goofing around and eat some.

**Diamonds are a girl's best friend.
But they don't taste good.**

Chocoholic Reasonettes

If not for chocolate,
there would be no need
for control top pantyhose.
An entire garment industry
would be devastated.

160

Chocoholic Reasonettes

Without ample chocolate consumption, all those diet book guys would be homeless.

161

Chocoholic Reasonettes

You might be a chocoholic if:
you stash chocolate in
different rooms so you're
never far from it.

Chocoholic Reasonettes

Any second, a huge meteor
could strike the planet and
you'd wish you had eaten
more chocolate.

Chocoholic Reasonettes

**Chocolate won't leave
nicotine stains
on your teeth.**

164

Chocoholic Reasonettes

**Eat chocolate.
Go with what you know.**

165

Chocoholic Reasonettes

Put 'eat chocolate' at the top
of your list of things to do today.
That way, at least you'll get one thing done.

Chocolate is always in season.

Other Titles By Great Quotations

301 Ways to Stay Young At Heart
African-American Wisdom
A Lifetime of Love
A Light Heart Lives Long
A Servant's Heart
A Teacher Is Better Than Two books
A Touch of Friendship
Angle-grams
As A Cat Thinketh
Astrology for Cats
Astrology for Dogs
Can We Talk
Celebrating Women
Chicken Soup
Chocoholic Reasonettes
Daddy & Me
Erasing My Sanity
Fantastic Father, Dependable Dad
Golden Years, Golden Words
Graduation Is Just The Beginning
Grandma, I Love You
Happiness Is Found Along The Way
High Anxieties
Hooked on Golf

I Didn't Do it
Ignorance Is Bliss
I'm Not Over the Hill
Inspirations
Interior Design for Idiots
Let's Talk Decorating
Life's Lessons
Life's Simple Pleasures
Looking for Mr. Right
Midwest Wisdom
Mother, I Love You
Motivating Quotes,
 for Motivated People
Mommy & Me
Mrs. Murphy's Laws
Mrs. Webster's Dictionary
My Daughter,
 My Special Friend
Only A Sister
Parenting 101
Pink Power
Reflections
Romantic Rhapsody
Social Disgraces

Someone Pleeease pull
 The Fire Alarm!
Stress or Sanity
TeenAge of Insanity
Thanks From The Heart
The ABC's of Parenting
The Be-Attitudes
The Cornerstone of Success
The Lemonade Handbook
The Mother Load
The Other Species
The Rose Mystique
The Secrets in Your face
The Secrets in Your Name
The Secret Language of men
The Secret Language of
 Women
The Sports Page
Things You'll Learn...
Wedding Wonders
Word From The Coach
Working Woman's World

Great Quotations, Inc.
8102 Lemont Road,
#300, Woodridge, IL 60517
Phone: 630-390-3580   Fax: 630-390-3585